Drama for Students, Volume 2

McNeil, Gary Oudersluys, Maureen Richards, *Research Specialists*
Julia C. Daniel, Tamara C. Nott, Tracie A. Richardson, Cheryl L. Warnock, *Research Associates*

Susan M. Trosky, *Permissions Manager*
Kimberly F. Smilay, *Permissions Specialist*
Sarah Chesney, *Permissions Associate*
Steve Cusack, Kelly A. Quin, *Permissions Assistants*

Mary Beth Trimper, *Production Director*
Evi Seoud, *Assistant Production Manager*
Shanna Heilveil, *Production Assistant*

Randy Bassett, *Image Database Supervisor*
Mikal Ansari, Robert Duncan, *Imaging Specialists*
Pamela A. Reed, *Photography Coordinator*

Cynthia Baldwin, *Product Design Manager*
Cover design: Michelle DiMercurio, *Art Director*
Page design: Pamela A. E. Galbreath, *Senior Art Director*

This book is printed on acid-free paper that meets the minimum requirements of American National Standard for Information Sciences—Permanence Paper for Printed Library Materials, ANSI Z39.48-1984.

ISBN 0-7876-1684-2

ISSN applied for and pending
Printed in the United States of America
10 9 8 7 6 5 4 3

The Odd Couple

Neil Simon 1965

Introduction

When *The Odd Couple* appeared on Broadway in March of 1965, Neil Simon was already a fairly well-known playwright. His successful comedy, *Come Blow Your Horn,* had initiated his Broadway career in 1961 and *Barefoot in the Park* in 1963 had been an even bigger hit. But *The Odd Couple,* with its unforgettable pair of mismatched roommates, made Simon a cultural phenomenon, and he subsequently became in his own lifetime the most commercially successful playwright in the history of theatre. After its long run on Broadway, *The Odd*

Couple was turned into a successful film in 1968 and then became a popular television series (on the American Broadcasting Company network) running from 1970 to 1975. Thus, Oscar Madison and Felix Ungar, the "odd couple" of the title, were steadily prominent in the popular entertainment industry for ten years and, as a result, became a part of American culture. Though some may forget which one was "sloppy" and which one "neat," almost everyone understands the phrase "odd couple" as a way of describing a mismatched pair. The television show is still syndicated in reruns, the movie version appears frequently on television, and regional and local theatre groups mount productions of the play with great regularity. In 1985 Simon responded to the continued popularity of his odd pair by writing a female version for Broadway, in which all the characters' genders were reversed. Though not as popular as the original play, this new version helped perpetuate the "odd couple" as one of the most memorable pair of characters in the history of commercial theatre.

Author Biography

Neil Simon was born on July 4, 1927, in the Bronx, New York, the younger son of a father who sold cloth fabric to the dress manufacturers in Manhattan's garment district. At the age of fifteen Simon teamed with his older brother Danny to write comedy sketches for the annual employee party of a Brooklyn department store; their success in this endeavor convinced Simon that he wanted to be a comedy writer. He and Danny eventually wrote sketches for popular radio and television shows, but the partnership split in 1954 and Neil went on to write for television comedians like Sid Caesar, Garry Moore, Phil Silvers, Red Buttons, and Jerry Lewis.

Though successful enough to earn two Emmy Awards for television writing in 1957 and 1959, Simon found writing for television unfulfilling and in the fall of 1957 began working, in his spare time, on his first play. *Come Blow Your Horn,* based on his relationship with Danny and their parents, took him three years to write, and he went through twenty-two completely different versions. When the finished *Come Blow Your Horn* finally appeared on Broadway in 1961, however, its success launched Simon's playwriting career. His second comedy, *Barefoot in the Park* (1963), was based on the life he and his first wife, Joan Baim, had lived in a small apartment in New York City's Greenwich Village. With a young Robert Redford in one of the lead roles this comedy was even more successful than his first. In his third and most famous comedy, *The Odd Couple,* Danny served as the model for the meticulous Felix Ungar. By all standards, the play was an enormous success. By the mid-1960s Neil Simon was rich, successful, and very famous. He was so prolific with his comedy hits in the late 1960s and early 1970s that he sometimes had as many as four shows running simultaneously on Broadway.

In 1973, Joan, Simon's wife of twenty years, died of cancer. Simon subsequently married actress Marsha Mason, who would star in several productions of his work. His *Chapter Two* (1977) was based on Simon's complex emotional response to Joan's death and his second marriage. While still a comedy, this play represents a turning point in Simon's career, introducing more serious shadings to his palette. Many of his subsequent plays adopted this new pattern and from 1983 to 1986 a trilogy of such autobiographical plays—*Brighton Beach Memoirs, Biloxi Blues,* and *Broadway Bound* — won Simon greater praise from critics. In the 1990s, his fourth decade of play writing, Simon's success continued, and in 1996 he published the first half of his memoirs, *Rewrites,* which covers the period from his birth to the reception of *Chapter Two.*

Plot Summary

Act I: The Initial Poker Game

The Odd Couple opens on a hot summer night in the large, twelfth-floor apartment of New York City sportswriter Oscar Madison. A few months earlier, before Oscar's wife left him, the apartment had reflected the modest luxury of its Riverside Drive neighborhood on the Upper East Side of Manhattan. But the apartment is now a mess because Oscar is very sloppy and his weekly poker game is in progress. Dirty dishes, empty bottles, half-filled glasses, ashtrays, and other messes created by the poker game have been added to the discarded clothes, old newspapers, magazines, mail, and disarrayed furniture that are part of Oscar's everyday sloppiness.

As the curtain rises on this smoke-filled room we see Murray, Roy, Speed, and Vinnie around the poker table. They are concerned about the unusual lateness of one of their regular poker players, Felix Ungar. Oscar enters from the kitchen with food for his buddies, the phone rings. It's Oscar's wife complaining about his overdue alimony payments. Two more phone calls, one from Murray's wife and another to Felix's wife, Frances, inform everyone that Felix is missing because earlier in the day his wife declared an end to their twelve-year marriage. The poker players worry that the sensitive Felix might be contemplating suicide, and when he finally arrives at Oscar's apartment they try to pretend that everything is normal while simultaneously interpreting everything Felix does as a preamble to suicide. Felix admits that earlier in the day he swallowed a whole bottle of pills but then vomited them up. After heartfelt expressions of concern, Murray, Roy, Speed, and Vinnie go home, and Oscar tries to console Felix, massaging his neck and back, pouring him a drink. When Felix hums and hops from leg to leg, bellowing like a moose to clear his ears, we get an indication of the eccentricity that might have led his wife to expel him. Felix confesses that he was unbearably obsessive about such things as petty finances, cleaning house, and cooking. Oscar sympathizes by describing the traits that led his wife to leave him. He invites Felix to move in with him, admitting that he doesn't like living alone. Felix agrees, imagining all the ways he can help Oscar—from fixing things to cooking and cleaning. During this discussion, Felix's wife calls but only to find out when Felix is coming back for his clothes (she wants to have the bedroom repainted). Felix declares his acceptance of the failed marriage and starts to clean up Oscar's apartment, responding to Oscar's goodnight by calling Oscar by his wife's name, Frances.

Act II, Scene 1: The Second Poker Game

Two weeks later, about eleven at night, another

poker game is in session, but this time the apartment is immaculately clean. Felix appears from the kitchen with carefully prepared food and reminds all the players to use their coasters to preserve the carefully applied finish on the table. Some of the players, like Vinnie, are quite pleased with the new atmosphere. Others, like Oscar and Speed, are aggravated by the excessive concern for tidiness. The game breaks up prematurely and Murray is the last to leave, commenting on how happy he thinks Oscar and Felix must be living the bachelor life. But in the argument that ensues following Murray's departure, Oscar makes it clear that he is very unhappy living with the excessively tidy Felix. He asserts that Felix is obsessive about controlling things, including his own emotions, and ought to loosen up, relax, and have more fun. But when Felix tries to express his anger by throwing a cup against the door, he hurts his shoulder. Oscar's plan for loosening up and having more fun is to invite to dinner two attractive sisters from the upstairs apartment. Gwendolyn and Cecily Pigeon are British (they say "solicitor" instead of "lawyer"). Oscar met them on the elevator a week earlier, and he is eager to get to know them better. Felix, however, feels a loyalty to his estranged wife that makes "dating" seem wrong to him. Following an argument, Felix finally relents and agrees to help entertain the Pigeon sisters— provided he can cook the dinner. He calls his wife to ask for her recipe for London broil.

Act II, Scene 2: An Evening with the Pigeon Sisters

A few days later, about eight at night, the dining room table is set elegantly for four. Felix is in the kitchen when Oscar enters cheerily. But Felix is angry because Oscar had told him he would be home at seven and that the sisters would arrive by seven-thirty. The dinner, planned for eight o'clock, is nearly ruined. Gwendolyn and Cecily arrive and they all sit, but Felix does not join the conversation until he comments, quite inappropriately, on the weather. When Oscar goes into the kitchen to fix drinks, Felix becomes the center of attention for the Pigeon sisters and tells them how much he misses his wife and children. This is not what Oscar had in mind for trying to romance the women, but Gwendoyn and Cecily find Felix "sensitive." When Oscar comes from the kitchen with their drinks all three are crying. Felix rushes into the kitchen to inspect his burned London broil and when he dejectedly returns, Gwendolyn and Cecily suggest that they all go upstairs to their apartment for dinner. The sisters leave to prepare but Felix tells Oscar he won't go because it would mean being unfaithful to his wife and children. Oscar goes upstairs alone, angrily accusing Felix of being unwilling to change, suggesting sarcastically that if he wants to commit suicide the apartment is indeed twelve floors from the pavement.

Act III: The Last Poker Game

The next evening, about seven-thirty, the apartment is set up for yet another poker game. Felix is vacuuming when Oscar comes in, still angry about the previous evening's failure with the Pigeon sisters. They argue and Oscar begins to sabatoge Felix's efforts at cleaning, finally throwing a plate of linguini against the kitchen wall. Oscar gets Felix's suitcase and demands that Felix move out. Felix leaves just as the other poker players arrive. His friends are worried about him but have started to play poker nonetheless. The doorbell rings and Gwendolyn, Cecily, and Felix appear. They have come for Felix's things because he is going to move in with the Pigeon sisters for a few days until he gets settled. Oscar and Felix shake hands just as Oscar's wife calls on the phone. Oscar sent her money to pay all his alimony, and he expresses a desire to talk with her again. As he is going out the door, Felix promises to come back for the next week's poker game. The poker game begins and Oscar admonishes the players to be careful of their cigarette butts.

Characters

Oscar Madison

Oscar Madison is the "messy" half of this famous "odd couple." Oscar takes pity on his best friend, the newly separated and nearly suicidal Felix Ungar, and invites Felix to live with him in his New York City apartment. Within two weeks, however, Oscar regrets the invitation. The 43-year-old Oscar is carefree, pleasant, and very appealing as a character. When asked by one of the poker players what kind of sandwiches he's serving, Oscar looks under the bread and says, "I got brown sandwiches and green sandwiches." The green, he says, is "either very new cheese or very old meat." At the end of the play there is a suggestion that Oscar's experience with Felix has provoked a change in his personality because Oscar's last words in the play are an admonishment to the poker players to be less messy. In both the original Broadway stage production in 1965 and in the movie version of 1968, Oscar was played by Walter Matthau. In the five-year television series beginning in 1970, Oscar was played by Jack Klugman.

Media Adaptations

- *The Odd Couple* was adapted by Simon himself as a 1968 film starring Walter Matthau as Oscar and Jack Lemmon as Felix. Gene Saks, who directed the stage version, also directed the film—which is very faithful to the play script, though occasionally expanded to include street scenes in New York City. In technicolor, running 106 minutes, available from Paramount Home Video and at many video rental stores. A videodisc (Laservision) version is also available from Paramount.
- An animated cartoon called *The Oddball Couple* premiered in September of 1976 on ABC and was

based on the odd couple concept as it featured a slob-like dog named Fleabag and a fussy cat named Spiffy, both freelance magazine writers.

- *The Odd Couple* was adapted as a 30 minute television show that ran on ABC from September of 1970 to July of 1975 and included 114 episodes. Jack Klugman played Oscar and Tony Randall played Felix, but in the series many other characters—like Oscar's secretary, Myrna, and Felix's daughter, Edna —had to be invented to satisfy the need for greater variety. Available in reruns on some cable television channels like Nickelodeon.
- *The Odd Couple* was adapted again by ABC in October of 1982 as another 30 minute television series called *The New Odd Couple* and ran until June of 1983 with black actors Demond Wilson and Ron Glass playing Oscar and Felix. Most episodes were simply recast versions of previous *The Odd Couple* scripts.

Murray

Murray, one of the poker players, is a

policeman and a methodical, even slow, thinker. He is also very gentle and caring, and demonstrates the most concern for Felix. Murray is fairly unflappable, but he is also a bit simple and naive.

Cecily Pigeon

Cecily Pigeon is a little more uninhibited than her sister, Gwendolyn; she is the one who makes such suggestive remarks as, "Oh, we've done spectacular things but I don't think we'd want it spread all over the telly."

Gwendolyn Pigeon

Though the Pigeon sisters seem almost indistinguishable, Simon describes Gwendolyn as the "mother hen." Like her sister Cicely, Gwendolyn is in her 30s, British, attractive, and works as a secretary for the Slenderama Health Club. She is a little slower mentally than her sister —she has trouble remembering Felix's name.

Roy

Roy is Oscar's accountant and a man with an acute sense of smell. He is the poker player who complains most about air quality and bad odors in Oscar's apartment. In the second act he storms from the game because the fastidious Felix has put disinfectant on the playing cards.

Speed

As his name implies, Speed is always in a hurry. He is the impatient poker player —sarcastic, complaining, and even a little mean. As the curtain rises on Murray shuffling the cards with agonizing slowness, the caustic Speed has the play's sharp first line: "Tell me, Mr. Maverick, is this your first time on the riverboat?"

Felix Ungar

Felix Ungar is the "neat" member of the "odd couple," originally played on Broadway by Art Carney (he also played the character Norton on the popular Jackie Gleason television comedy *The Honeymooners*). In the movie, the role was rendered by Jack Lemmon, and in the television series Tony Randall portrayed Felix. A 44-year-old news writer for CBS, Felix responds to his wife's decision to end their marriage by considering suicide, but in Simon's comic world, attempted suicide is funny rather than serious; the compulsively tidy Felix sends his suicide note to his wife in a telegram. Oscar claims that Felix's problem is an obsession with control and urges Felix to "let loose" once in a while, to do something he "feels" like doing rather than always doing what he thinks he's "supposed" to do. At the end of the play, when Felix accepts the invitation from the Pigeon sisters to stay in their apartment, he is perhaps demonstrating a less conventional aspect of his personality.

Vinnie

Vinnie, the last of the poker players, is nervous and eccentric. At the initial poker game he is constantly checking his watch because he wants to leave early—he's departing for a vacation in Florida (in July) the next morning.

Themes

Order and Disorder

When two good friends newly separated from their wives decide to live together, the arrangement fails miserably because the two friends have personal habits and domestic lifestyles that are diametrically opposed. Felix likes to live in an extremely ordered and tidy living space while Oscar not only tolerates living in disorder and messiness but even seems to prefer it.

Simon is more interested in creating compelling character types and raucous laughter than he is in investigating ideas, but to the extent that *The Odd Couple* deals with theme it focuses on the friction between radically different personalities. There is never a sense that either Oscar or Felix is "right" and the other is "wrong." They are simply different and attempting to live together was a bad idea. Oscar initiated the idea because he was lonely and concerned for Felix, but in his carefree approach to life he did not anticipate the conflict that should have been apparent from his knowledge of Felix's habits. Oscar describes Felix as "a panicky person" obsessed with controlling everything in his life. Specifically, Felix panics when he is confronted with disorder in any form, and he attempts to "fix" things by restoring his concept of order thus giving himself the illusion of control. When Felix accepts the invitation to live with Oscar, he characteristically adopts the very behavior patterns that drove his wife to dismiss him. At the end of Act I, Oscar repeatedly asks Felix to go to sleep, but Felix insists on staying up to clean, saying he needs pencil and paper "to start rearranging my life." He says,"I've got to get organized," and the malleable Oscar finally gives in. When Felix unconsciously calls Oscar "Frances," Felix's wife's name, it is clear that Felix is looking to Oscar as some sort of substitute for the relationship he had with his wife.

Public vs. Private Life

Oscar and Felix are best friends, but before moving in together they share only a public life with one another. When they finally share a living space, they discover that the pressures of private life are much more demanding. The transition from "good friends" to pseudo "husband and wife" tests compatibility in a way that only experience can prove. The same living space and the experience of round-the-clock sharing magnifies differences and makes the discord inescapable and intolerable. Oscar and Felix were certainly aware of their personality differences before they lived together, but they encountered these differences only briefly in their public relationship, largely at the Friday night poker game. In Act III, when Oscar throws Felix's suitcase on the table and insists that Felix leave, he says, "all I want is my freedom." Even with his unusual tolerance for disorder, Oscar cannot live in inescapable proximity with behavior that is so different from his own. He admits that it's not a question of right or wrong: "It's not your fault, Felix. It's a rotten combination."

Very clearly, Simon is suggesting that heterosexual marriages can also suffer from the same hopeless conflicts when they exchange a "public" relationship for an intimate and "private" one. Simon communicates this theme by drawing attention to the way the relationship between Oscar and Felix is very much like a marriage. In Act I, when Oscar is trying to convince Felix to take advantage of his offer, he says, "I'm proposing to you. What do you want, a ring?" In the second scene of Act II, Oscar and Felix sound like the cliched married couple when they argue—"If you knew you were going to be late, why didn't you call me?" Similarly, the opening of Act III, when Oscar and Felix are not "talking," perfectly mimics the archetypal marriage spat. When Oscar tells Felix he must leave, he says, "it's all over, Felix. The whole marriage. We're getting an annulment." And Felix responds, "Boy, you're in a bigger hurry than Frances was."

Topics for Further Study

- Compare the movie version of *The Odd Couple* with the television series. Which is more effective and why? How does each differ from the stage play?
- Research to discover how rising costs have affected Broadway and how economic pressures have contributed to the dichotomy between commercial entertainment and art in American theatre.
- Read several theoretical discussions that attempt to define comedy philosophically, as distinct from laughter, and then apply your definition of comedy to *The Odd Couple,* your favorite television sitcom, and to a Shakespearean

comedy.

- Identify the techniques that Simon uses in *The Odd Couple* to establish the conflict between Oscar and Felix by the end of Act I, to intensify that conflict in Acts II and III, and to resolve the conflict by the end of the play.

Simon strengthens this aspect of the theme by calling attention to the marital and near-marital relationships that surround Oscar and Felix. It's clear that Speed's marriage has its rocky moments because he compares the aggravation he feels in the poker game to the aggravation he gets at home. Murray responds to Oscar's pretending on the phone that he is having an affair with Murray's wife by saying, "I wish you *were* having an affair with her. Then she wouldn't bother *me* all the time." Murray perhaps speaks for the general skepticism about marriage by saying, "twelve years doesn't mean you're a *happy* couple. It just means you're a *long* couple." In contrast with these rocky relationships, Vinnie appears to have a happier marriage, dedicated as he is to his frequent travels with his wife. In direct contrast to Oscar and Felix, the Pigeon sisters seem to live together without serious conflict—perhaps because, unlike Oscar and Felix, they are so much alike.

Finally, Simon puts this theme into perspective by using the public relationships between the poker players as a backdrop for Oscar and Felix. The poker players meet once a week and as a result know one another well, but their apparent camaraderie is never tested by the more demanding situation of living together over a long period of time. And Simon is careful to show that their relationships are filled with potential conflict and tension due to personality differences. The irascible Speed, for example, seems always on the verge of quitting the group. But at the end, even Felix vows to come back to the next poker night. He's not going to "break up" the game because "marriages may come and go, but the game must go on."

Change and Transformation

The only way that marriages survive is through the compromise that must occur when inevitable conflicts arise. Oscar and Felix's experience shows that some conflicts are too great for compromise, but they point the way toward the necessity for compromise by demonstrating slight changes in their personalities by the end of the play. Oscar's change becomes clear when he receives a phone call from his ex-wife and reveals that he paid up his alimony in full. He says, "you don't have to thank me. I'm just doing what's right." Oscar's relationship with his wife and son appear to be improving because he has become a more responsible husband and father. And, of course, he ends the play with his admonition to the poker players to "watch your cigarettes, will you? This is my house, not a pig sty."

The change in Felix is much more mysterious. Moving in even temporarily with the Pigeon sisters, nearly total strangers, is something Felix would not have been able to do when the play began. But is he merely "loosening up" as Oscar suggested he ought to? Or is he making a huge change and considering a romantic relationship with either or both of the sisters? As he gathers his things in Oscar's apartment, Felix passes the poker players and smiles in a way that is open to interpretation. When he moves in with Gwendolyn and Cecily will he try to tidy up their lives the way he attacked Oscar's? There is no way to know, but it is clear that he has gone through some kind of change for he asks Murray to tell his wife that "if I sound different to her, it's because I'm not the same man she kicked out three weeks ago."

While the play's ending leaves Oscar and Felix's future relationship open to some speculation, it seems reasonable to assume that the two men will not live together again. It is interesting to note then, that the popular television series presumed a different scenario. In the television situation comedy version of *The Odd Couple,* Oscar and Felix remain roommates, each having reached a kind of mutual tolerance for the other's idiosyncracies. The series did, however, preserve much of the friction between the two characters, in order to maintain comical conflicts similar to the play. This is something of a reversal of Simon's suggested outcome, but one that can be seen as necessary to perpetuate a weekly comedic series.

Style

Conflict

In November of 1963, Simon sold the screen-rights for *The Odd Couple* to Paramount Pictures before he had even written a single word of the play upon which the movie was eventually based. In his memoir, *Rewrites,* Simon quotes the single sentence he and his agent used to close the deal: "'Well, it's about two men who are divorced, move in together to save money to pay their alimony, and have the same fights with each other as they did with their wives.'"

This anecdote illustrates the effectiveness of the play's main dramatic conflict. One sentence was all Paramount needed to know that Neil Simon could deliver another hit. The inherently funny conflict between the fussy Felix Ungar and the messy Oscar Madison is subtly established by the end of Act I, is effectively intensified in Act II and the beginning of Act III, and then finally is resolved by their separation and small changes in personality at the end of the play. The conflict is comically ironic because the solution the two men come up with for their separate divorces ends up creating yet another kind of divorce.

In Simon's memoir he recounts that the most difficult part of writing the play was writing the resolution of the conflict in Act III. From the beginning of the rehearsal period, it was clear that the first two acts were effective but that the third act was a disastrous failure. This last act did not get a satisfactory rewrite until well after the first out-of-town performances had begun and Simon had realized that the key to resolving the conflict was bringing the Pigeon sisters back into Act III.

Character

What was not obvious in Simon's one-sentence synopsis for Paramount is that the conflict was based on the clash of extremely different personality types. Ultimately, it is the creation of Oscar and Felix as an "oil and water" mix that makes it possible for *The Odd Couple* to be tremendously funny.

Simon creates these contrasting character types with the effective use of theatrical detail, most notably with carefully crafted dialogue. Sometimes it is the words of the character himself that establishes the "type" as when when Oscar enters hurriedly in Act I carrying a tray with beer, sandwiches, a can of peanuts, and already opened bags of pretzels and chips. In the visual context of the slovenly apartment, Oscar's balancing act with the snacks already characterizes him as the probable source of the living room mess but his opening words very subtly reinforce this impression. The impatient poker players ask Oscar if he's "in" or "out," that is, whether or not he plans to play this hand. "I'm in! I'm in!" Oscar says, "Go ahead.

Deal!" Vinnie asks,"Aren't you going to look at your cards?" and Oscar answers, "What for? I'm gonna bluff anyway." The messy condition of Oscar's apartment has prepared the audience to understand his carefree type immediately, and his opening words characterize him perfectly with elegant economy.

Sometimes Felix and Oscar are effectively characterized by what others say about them. The third line of the play, for example, is Roy's "Geez, it stinks in here," a line that is quickly followed by Vinnie's,"What time is it?" Roy's line implies that the yet-to-appear host is the main cause of the mess they find themselves in, an impression he solidifies with a later line, "You know, it's the same garbage from last week's game. I'm beginning to recognize things." Felix doesn't enter until nearly half-way through the first act, but when he does the following comment from Murray has already characterized Felix as one who organizes his life in a way very unlike Oscar—"Hey, maybe he's in his office locked in the john again. Did you know Felix was once locked in the john overnight. He wrote out his entire will on a half a roll of toilet paper! Heee, what a nut!"

As fictional creations, Oscar and Felix, like the other characters in the play, are "types" rather than multifaceted characters. They mostly embody single, predominating traits—as in Oscar the carefree, irresponsible, and sloppy type and Felix the precise, uptight, and extremely orderly type. Multifaceted characters are generally considered more artistically sophisticated, but character "types" can be used to great artistic purpose, as in the novels of Charles Dickens for example. Simon draws his character types precisely, using carefully crafted dialogue to reveal their characteristics.

Comedy

When one thinks of comedy one thinks first of laughter, and the *The Odd Couple* generates belly laughs, mainly because of the verbal cleverness captured in its "one-liners." The "one-liner" is a short response in which the character's retort surprises because of exaggeration or incongruity. For example, when Murray agrees to eat the "brown" sandwich that Oscar brings out of the kitchen, Roy says, "are you crazy? His refrigerator's been broken for two weeks. I saw milk standing in there that wasn't even in the bottle." The laugh comes from the surprising and exaggerated image of milk so sour it has become a solid substance. Simon perfected his skill at one-liners writing for television shows in the 1950s and no dramatist has ever been more adept at this skill. It has, however, been something of a hindrance to his reputation as a serious artist. Though audiences have been enthusiastic in their response to Simon's comedies, critics have generally been less admiring, often citing the reliance on "one-liners" as a cheap trick more appropriate to the world of sitcom entertainment than the world of art.

Historical Context

Vietnam

1965 was a period of considerable turmoil in the United States because President Lyndon Johnson, despite his claims to the contrary, was escalating U.S. involvement in Vietnam and many citizens (mostly young people) were protesting, especially on college campuses around the nation. In February, a month before *The Odd Couple* opened on Broadway in March, U.S. bombers were retaliating against North Vietnamese forces for attacks on American military advisors in South Vietnam. By March the first deployment of U.S. combat troops was landing in Da Nang and student protests had begun to mushroom. In May, a nation-wide student protest including more than 100 U.S. colleges proclaimed its opposition to the war. Despite this public outcry, Congress authorized the use of U.S. ground troops in direct combat operations and by the end of June full-scale combat involving American troops had commenced. Continued anti-war rallies ultimately divided the American public between "hawks" and "doves," those who supported the escalation of the war and those who opposed it. Often these lines divided on grounds of age and education, with college faculty and students usually leading the ranks of the "doves." As draft calls were doubled to enlist troops for Vietnam, university enrollments rose sharply with young men taking advantage of the draft deferral for college students as a way of avoiding military service.

Racial tensions

Adding to the turmoil created by Vietnam were continuing tensions over race relations. In Selma, Alabama, throughout February and March, Martin Luther King Jr. was leading civil rights protests against state regulations that limited black voter registration. Demonstrations were marred by violence as 200 Alabama state police used whips, night sticks, and tear gas to control the largely black crowds. The Governor of Alabama at the time, George Wallace, finally refused police protection for the demonstrators and President Johnson responded by sending 3,000 U.S. National Guard troops to Selma. Elsewhere, in New York City's Harlem, on February 21, civil rights activist Malcolm X was assassinated by black extremists as he prepared to deliver a speech asserting the need for peaceful coexistence between blacks and whites. In the Watts section of Los Angeles in August, race riots erupted in this predominantly black section of the city and nearly 10,000 rioters destroyed 500 square blocks of the city and caused an estimated $40 million of damage. In 1965, race relations in America were obviously volatile and even dangerous to peace and public safety.

- **1965:** The divorce rate stood at 2.5% per 1,000 people, down from its high after World War II but up from a lower rate in 1960. The divorce rate had risen from 0.9% in 1910 and had jumped dramatically during the second World War to 3.5% in 1945, peaking in 1946 after the war had ended but then dipping steadily to 2.2% in 1960.

  Today: The divorce rate stands at around 4.6% per 1,000 people, down from its all-time high of 5.3% in 1981. The rates had risen steadily from 1965 and into the 1970s before peaking and starting another decline in the mid 1980s.

- **1965:** The issue of racial prejudice dominated the news and the social consciences of the American people, but there was no evidence of black characters in the lives of Oscar, Felix, or their poker-playing buddies. The issues of gender consciousness and homophobia were much less prominent, and, in this social climate, few, if any, considered it homoerotically suggestive that two bachelors chose to live together.

  Today: Though the issue of racial prejudice is still very much "in the air," it has now been joined or even eclipsed in importance by the issues of feminism and homophobia. Increased awareness of gay issues has made many people more observant of homosexual subtext, and the relationship between Oscar and Felix can, on some levels, be perceived as homoerotic. The feminist movement can also be seen as a factor in Simon's decision to create a "female" version of the play in 1985. In 1982, ABC produced a second sitcom version of the play that featured black actors in the roles of Oscar and Felix.

- **1965:** America was becoming deeply mired in the Vietnam conflict and open hostilities at home over the war would dominate the rest of the decade, culminating in the National Guard opening fire on Kent State University student protestors, killing four and wounding eight on May 4, 1970.

  Today: The memories of Vietnam still weigh heavily on America's psyche, though the 1991 Persian Gulf War was seen by many as a ritualistic military victory that in part exorcised the ignominy of that earlier military failure. Novels, plays, and popular films about Vietnam began appearing in the mid

1970s and became so numerous in the 1980s and 1990s that an entire genre of Vietnam War literature has arisen.

- **1965:** The "cold war" begun in the early 1950s was still raging and Communist Russia was seen as a great and dangerous political and military power.
  Today: The fall of the Berlin Wall in November of 1989 signaled the economic and political decline of Russia, which is now splintered into many independent states and is suffering from internal dissension and severe economic problems as it attempts to assimilate the Western concepts of democracy and free market capitalism.

- **1965:** Stock prices and trading volume reached an all-time high, with the Dow-Jones industrial average gaining about 11% in 1965 to finish the year at a historic high of 969.
  Today: After a major "crash" in 1987, the stock market continues to climb to dizzying heights, fueled by "baby-boomer" investors who worry that they will not have sufficient funds for retirement. In the greatest "bull" run in the history of the

market, the Dow-Jones industrial average flirted with the 7,000 mark and some analysts predicted a 10,000 point Dow by the year 2000 while others predicted another crash of monumental proportions.

- **1965:** Simon's opening allusion to "Mr. Maverick" was funny for his audience because the hit television series starring James Garner and Jack Kelly as Bret and Bart Maverick had just ended its 124 episode run on ABC in 1962.
  Today: A new generation has become familiar with the Maverick character through the popular 1994 movie starring Mel Gibson as Bret Maverick and Jodi Foster as his spunky romantic interest. James Garner, the original Bret Maverick, took a supporting role in the film as Marshal Zane Cooper and lent considerable nostalgia to the film for an older generation of viewers.

"Flower Power"

An idealistic youth culture in America responded to this turmoil by asserting its belief in the power of a non-denominational spiritual awareness. Poet Allen Ginsberg coined the term "flower power" when anti-war demonstrators responded to Oakland city police with a strategy of non-violence. Images of young people inserting daisies in the barrels of police anti-riot weapons helped popularize the epithet. Identifying more with Eastern religions than with traditional Christianity, these "flower children" embraced "love" and "peace" as attainable foundations for social and political order. This movement was led by "gurus" like Ginsberg, the Hare Krishnas, and Harvard psychology professor Timothy Leary, who espoused the use of consciousness-altering drugs such as LSD and marijuana.

The Insulated World of Simon's Play

As with most of his comedies, Simon's *The Odd Couple* is not seriously concerned with the social, political, and cultural climate of the times in which he wrote. Simon admits that he is not a "political" writer but said in *Rewrites:* "[I] hope that my plays become a documentation of the times we lived in, at least from the perspective I had to view it all." *The Odd Couple* might document an upper-middle-class New Yorker's world in 1965 but it would certainly be a very insulated world, quite unconnected to the significant turmoil most of the country was experiencing outside of Oscar's apartment.

It is most likely that this insulated quality derives from Simon's dedication to light, comedic entertainment, a desire to provide the audience with an engaging but untroubling evening of laughter and sentiment. In fact, *The Odd Couple* might even have been designed to provide its audience with an escape from the sometimes gruesome realities that were taking place on the street and being reported on the evening news. As with most of Simon's comedies, *The Odd Couple* is a pleasant night in the theatre rather than a disturbing or even thought-provoking one. Its most "serious" issue is divorce, and, in the spirit of light comedy, divorce is treated as a human experience without significantly troubling consequences or ramifications.

Critical Overview

The Odd Couple has been Neil Simon's greatest popular success, running for 964 performances in its Broadway debut and then spawning a popular movie version, an even more popular television series, and eventually a kind of sequel or "female version" that tells the same story with the genders reversed. Added to these successes is the fact that all of these manifestations of his play have entertained the public for more than thirty years as regional and amateur theatre groups continue to perform both versions of his play and television stations rerun the movie and sitcom series. But Simon has always been more popular with audiences than he has been with critics—who tend to classify him as a merely entertaining comedy writer rather than as a serious artist with a comic vision.

In 1965, *The Odd Couple* was Simon's third straight comedy hit (the 1962 musical *Little Me* had been less successful with audiences despite Simon's collaboration as librettist). The critics had responded in 1961 to his first Broadway hit, *Come Blow Your Horn,* with reserved praise, finding it (in *New York Times* critic Howard Taubman's words) a pleasant "confection," a play with "hilarious moments" that "aims low" and only seeks "to entertain." This would become the general critical opinion of Simon's work throughout his career, as his next two hits, *Barefoot in the Park* and *The Odd*

Couple, gathered basically similar responses. Through succeeding decades the critical response might vary slightly from play to play but the overall assessment stayed roughly the same. Consistently recognized as a sound theatrical craftsman and a genuinely funny writer, the critics nonetheless found Simon lacking in intellectual and emotional depth and often reduced him to the simple epithet, "gag-man."

Reviewing the original Broadway production of *The Odd Couple,* Taubman found the opening scene "one of the funniest card sessions ever held on a stage" and the play's humor "unflagging" but labelled the play finally as a "farce," and not of the "higher art" of "true comedy." Taubman's appreciation of the play's hilarity was thorough and genuine but he finally had to separate himself from the audience's more unreserved applause.

Some critics, like Walter Kerr, have been kinder to Simon during his career; Kerr, for example, once called Simon "a man of sense, using just the jigger and a half of substance that will make a decent drink." Other critics, like subsequent *Times* writers Frank Rich and John Simon (no relation), have been generally harsher. John Simon once proclaimed that Neil Simon's work was "devoid of ideas" and "an outrage . . . against human intelligence and art." He admitted that "audiences, of course, may find trash to their taste; but the critic's first task is to identify it as such. Then, if people still want to eat it, let them; only let no one pretend it's food." Academicians have generally been harshest of all when they deign to comment on such a popular writer. College and university professors well-studied in classic comic dramatists like Shakespeare and Moliere (pronounced "Mole-yair") and even more contemporary writers like Alan Ayckbourn (pronounced "ache-born") and Joe Orton have often been brutal with Simon. For example, in the third edition of *Contemporary Dramatists,* Martin Gottfried admits that "Neil Simon must be reckoned with if only because he is the most popular playwright in the history of the American theatre" but adds that "Simon is generally dismissed as a hack." Similarly, Gerald Berkowitz, writing in *Players* magazine begins by declaiming that "Neil Simon is a critical embarrassment. . . it is universally agreed that [his plays] offer no specific insights into the human condition." But even critics as harsh as these must admit to certain strengths in Simon's comedies, most notably the indisputable fact "that a Neil Simon comedy makes the audiences laugh, and [that] this laughter is louder, longer and more constant than that produced by any other modern dramatist," according to Berkowitz.

On the other hand, Simon has had his champions. In fact, two book-length critical assessments of his work are both quite effusive in their praise. Edythe McGovern, in her *Neil Simon: A Critical Study,* puts Simon in a class with writers like Moliere and George Bernard Shaw, who "successfully raised fundamental and sometimes tragic issues of universal and therefore enduring interest without eschewing the comic mode." Of *The Odd Couple* McGovern asserts that Simon has "captured the essence of incompatibility among humans who repeat again and again their self-defeating patterns of personality." In *Neil Simon,* Robert Johnson asserts that "Neil Simon has not received as much critical attention as he deserves," and that "Simon's work also explores a larger number of serious themes and points of view than he is credited with presenting." Johnson concludes that "Oscar and Felix's attempt to share living quarters. . . is the most captivating dramatization of incongruity Simon has yet created."

The individual interested in Neil Simon's comedies can come to his or her own opinion about the merit of Simon's comedy or about *The Odd Couple* in particular by seeking out learned definitions of comedy and comparing them to a multitude of works in literature and in the popular media.

What Do I Read Next?

- Any of the plays of Britain's Alan Ayckbourn, who is often referred to as the "British Neil Simon" because of his commercial popularity, his ability to create laughter, and his prolific number of hits. More respected by critics, Ayckbourn is signficantly more daring technically and much more profound in his use of comedy than Simon.
- *Taking Laughter Seriously,* by John Morreall, SUNY Press, 1983. A concise discussion of the psychological elements that underlie laughter, with a concluding chapter discussing humor as a way of looking at life.
- *The Gingerbread Lady* (1970), *God's Favorite* (1974), *Chapter Two* (1977), or *Lost in Yonkers* (1991) as examples of Neil Simon plays that work with darker materials and make more of an attempt to balance humor with seriousness.
- *The Sunshine Boys* (1972) for another fascinating Neil Simon "pair," this time two, old, vaudevillian comics who have a love-hate relationship with one another.

Further Reading

Bryer, Jackson R., editor. *The Playwright's Art: Conversations with Contemporary Dramatists,* Rutgers University Press, 1995, pp. 221-240.

Interview with Simon responding to questions as varied as "how did you get started writing plays?" to "how do you feel about theatre critics?"

Johnson, Robert K. *Neil Simon,* Twayne, 1983.

The second and currently last book devoted to Simon's work; includes chapter on *The Odd Couple*.

McGovern, Edythe. *Neil Simon: A Critical Study,* Frederick Ungar, 1978.

First book-length discussion of Simon; includes chapter on *The Odd Couple*.

Simon, Neil. *Rewrites,* Simon & Schuster, 1996.

Simon's autobiography through his writing of *Chapter Two*. Offers some interesting insights into his inspirations and writing processes.

Weise, Judith. "Neil Simon," in *Critical Survey of Drama: English Language Series,* edited by Frank N. Magill, Salem Press, 1985.

An insightful analysis of Simon's

comedies in general (through *Biloxi Blues)* including perceptive commentary on *The Odd Couple*.

Sources

Berkowitz, Gerald M. "Neil Simon and His Amazing Laugh Machine," *Players Magazine,* Vol. 47, no. 3, February-March, 1972, pp. 110-113.

Gottfried, Martin. "Simon, (Marvin) Neil," in *Contemporary Dramatists,* 3rd edition, St. Martin's Press, 1982.

Kerr, Walter. "A Jigger and a Half" in his *Thirty Plays Hath November,* Simon & Schuster, 1969, pp. 297-301.

Konas, Gary, editor. *Neil Simon: A Casebook,* Garland, 1997.

Simon, John. "Bad Things" in *New York,* January 13, 1975, pp. 54-55.

Taubman, Howard. Review of *Come Blow Your Horn* in the *New York Times,* February 23, 1961, p. 31.

Taubman, Howard. Reviews of *The Odd Couple* in the *New York Times,* March 9, 1965, p. 50; March 21, 1965, p. 1.

Milton Keynes UK
Ingram Content Group UK Ltd.
UKHW020716201124
2986UKWH00040B/473

9 781375 385428